Earth

N O T E S

Exploring the Southwest's
Canyon Country from the Airwaves

From the popular KNAU public radio show

Edited by Peter Friederici
Illustrated by Diane Iverson
Foreword by Gary Paul Nabhan

Grand Canyon Association
PO Box 399, Grand Canyon, AZ 86023-0399
(800) 858-2808
www.grandcanyon.org

KNAU/Arizona Public Radio
PO Box 5764, Flagstaff, AZ 86011-5764
(928) 523-5628
www.knau.org

Center for Sustainable Environments
PO Box 5765, Flagstaff, AZ 86011-5765
(928) 523-0637
www.environment.nau.edu

11   10   09   08   07   06   05   1   2   3   4   5   6   7

ISBN: 0-938216-84-8

Library of Congress Cataloging-in-Publication Data

Earth notes : exploring the Southwest's Canyon Country from the airwaves: from the popular KNAU public radio show / edited by Peter Friederici ; foreword by Gary Paul Nabhan.

p.   cm.

ISBN 0-938216-84-8 (alk. paper)

1.   Southwest, New--Description and travel. 2.   Arizona--Description and travel. 3.   Colorado Plateau--Description and travel. 4.   Natural history--Southwest, New. 5.   Natural history--Arizona. 6.   Natural history--Colorado Plateau. 7.   Southwest, New--Environmental conditions. 8.   Arizona--Environmental conditions. 9. Colorado Plateau--Environmental conditions. 10.   Earth notes (Radio program) I. Friederici, Peter, 1963- II. Nabhan, Gary Paul. III. Earth notes (Radio program)

F787.E23 2005
917.9--dc22
                          2005017976

Edited by Todd R. Berger
Designed by Ron Short

"Sand and Slickrock," "Seeps and Springs," "Aspens," "Salt," "Hogans," "Preserving Chimayó's Potreros," "Heirloom Seeds," and "Building with Straw" © 2005 by Richard Mahler. Reprinted by permission of the author.

"Volcanoes" © 2005 by Dennis Wall. Reprinted by permission of the author.

"How Canyons Grow" and "Return of the Condors" © 2005 by Anne Minard. Reprinted by permission of the author.

"The Poop on the Pleistocene" and "Steam Heat" © 2005 by Rose Houk. Reprinted by permission of the author.

"Monsoon Pollinators," "Cryptobiotic Crusts," "Piñon Pines," "Apaches and Wolves," and "Keeping the Night Sky Dark" © 2005 by Peter Friederici. Reprinted by permission of the author.

"Calendars of Stone" © 2005 by Bryan Bates. Reprinted by permission of the author.

"Changes in the Weather" © 2005 by Mary Tolan. Reprinted by permission of the author.

"Grizzly Bears" and "Rebuilding Adobes" © 2005 by Mona Mort. Reprinted by permission of the author.

"Fire Lookouts" and "Just Bad Luck?" © 2005 by Mike Lamp. Reprinted by permission of the author.

"Grand Canyon Hawks" © 2005 by John Grahame. Reprinted by permission of the author.

"Keeping Phantom Ranch Clean" and "Rescuing the Razorback Sucker" © 2005 by Terri Likens. Reprinted by permission of the author.

ACKNOWLEDGMENTS

Thanks to all of the people and organizations who have put *Earth Notes* on the air and made this book possible. Rob Elliott and Karan English were instrumental in conceptualizing and supporting the program. The *Earth Notes* production staff includes KNAU general manager John Stark and news director Mitch Teich; former development director Julie Pastrick helped gain underwriting support. Tristan Clum of KUNM narrates the show. Funding for *Earth Notes* has come from KNAU listeners; Arizona Raft Adventures; the City of Flagstaff Conservation Program; Coconino County, Arizona; the Elliott English Family Fund; Grand Canyon Trust; Flagstaff Cultural Partners; McCoy Motors; the Museum of Northern Arizona; NAU Center for Sustainable Environments; NAU Ecological Restoration Institute; T. Barnabas Kane & Associates; and Unisource.

Contents

FOREWORD

As I travel around northern Arizona and the greater Colorado Plateau, I frequently run into people who feel linked to one another through what some might assume to be an improbable connection: a brief but refreshing radio spot known as *Earth Notes*. They are connected, I believe, by a sense not only of concern but of hope about how people fit into the astonishing landscapes of the Southwest's canyon country. And those radio spots—like well-crafted haiku poems—move them toward a greater sense of wonder. Perhaps these reports from the field inspire them to participate in innovative ways to heal and revitalize our relationship with the earth.

Human interactions with the land, its vegetation, and its wildlife are obviously not all benign, but *Earth Notes* reminds us that there are many among us who have found ways to heal rather than further damage the places that we love. Sometimes a history lesson, at other times a look to the future, the stories broadcast on *Earth Notes* and printed in this book reinforce our sense of place, giving us "cultural antibodies" with which to resist detrimental change. But they also give us a new set of heroes: tradition-bearers and innovators who are making a tangible difference in this region and beyond.

As director of one of *Earth Notes*' cosponsors, the Center for Sustainable Environments, I am honored to know many of the behind-the-scenes contributors to the program and to this book. From the initial inspiration offered by Karan English and her comrades and the strong and consistent support of the KNAU staff, to the fine writing and editing of Peter Friederici and the silver voice of Tristan Clum, I am struck by how many diverse talents have coalesced to bring this effort to fruition. Let *Earth Notes* sing in your ears for many more years!

Gary Paul Nabhan
Director, Center for Sustainable Environments
Northern Arizona University
Flagstaff, Arizona

INTRODUCTION
SOMETHING IN THE AIR

The Colorado Plateau was the last blank spot to be filled in on the map of the contiguous United States. Cut off from the rest of North America by forbidding cliffs, mountains, canyons, and deserts, often presided over by punishing heat and aridity, it was hard to get to—or to leave. Even today it remains, in large part, a wild place, home to a remarkable diversity of natural communities—including a wide range of human cultures and languages—and to some of the cleanest air and broadest vistas on the continent. Its scenic wonders are instantly recognizable to visitors from around the world.

A great diversity of people live here, too. Though divided by rugged topography, distance, and artificial political boundaries, residents of the plateau possess a growing regional consciousness—*a sense of place*. Increasingly, they realize that air pollution, the distribution of water supplies, sustainability of crops, and the many other issues that govern the long-term health of the land and its communities affect all of us. These problems demand solutions that are inclusive, forward-thinking, and cooperative.

Since 2001 one of the significant agents of that growing regional consciousness has been something in the air: specifically, a short radio show called *Earth Notes*. Produced by KNAU/Arizona Public Radio and broadcast on a number of stations in the Four Corners region, *Earth Notes* takes listeners on a weekly tour of the Colorado Plateau. The program takes a look at the nature of the plateau, examines how people have historically dealt with its sometimes difficult conditions, and profiles innovative new strategies for sustainable living that people are putting into place—*this* place.

Earth Notes is smart, compelling, and hopeful. It is founded on the belief that people are shaped by their surroundings and that coming to terms with the conditions of a particular place is what molds human communities. It does not shy away from examining the serious environmental threats faced by communities on the Colorado Plateau, but it considers them opportunities, not just problems. Every week *Earth Notes* suggests new ways to appreciate and sustain the splendid surroundings of the upland Southwest. In this little book, we have collected some of the best *Earth Notes* scripts in order to profile the plateau, its people, and its possibilities.

At its heart, *Earth Notes* promotes the idea that living in a place is not just a matter of writing a particular zip code after one's return address. Rather, it involves learning the rhythms of climate, plants, and animals, and of the human communities that rely on those larger patterns. There is something in the air, all right, and it is showing us the way to a future in which people honor the environment they live in simply because it is home.

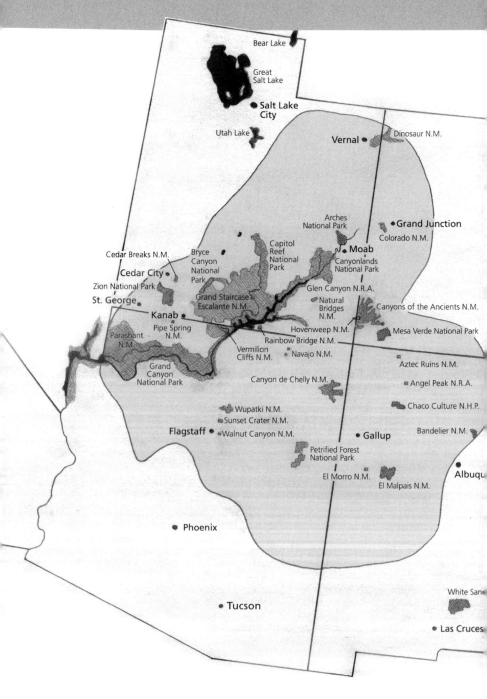

Bear Lake

Great
Salt Lake

● Salt Lake
City

Utah Lake

Vernal ●

Dinosaur N.M.

Arches
National Park

● Grand Junction

Colorado N.M.

Cedar Breaks N.M.

Bryce
Canyon
National
Park

Capitol
Reef
National
Park

● Moab

Canyonlands
National Park

Cedar City ●

Zion National Park

St. George ●

Grand Staircase–
Escalante N.M.

Glen Canyon N.R.A.

Natural
Bridges
N.M.

Canyons of the Ancients N.M.

Kanab ●

Pipe Spring
N.M.

Hovenweep N.M.

Mesa Verde National Park

Parashant
N.M.

Rainbow Bridge N.M.

Vermilion
Cliffs N.M.

Navajo N.M.

Aztec Ruins N.M.

Grand
Canyon
National
Park

Canyon de Chelly N.M.

Angel Peak N.R.A.

Wupatki N.M.

Chaco Culture N.H.P.

Sunset Crater N.M.

Flagstaff ●

Walnut Canyon N.M.

● Gallup

Bandelier N.M.

Petrified Forest
National Park

El Morro N.M.

El Malpais N.M.

Albuqu

● Phoenix

White San

● Tucson

● Las Cruces

Rocky Mountain
National Park

● Denver

● Colorado Springs

nta Fe

PART ONE
THE LAY OF THE LAND

Millions around the world know the Colorado Plateau as the world's greatest rock museum. It is the home address of countless hues of sandstone that memorialize vanished deserts and oceans, of limestones rich in the fossils of extinct sea creatures, of brittle volcanic lavas and cinders that poured forth in heat and violence, of the ancient and polished schists more than a billion years old that form the basement rocks of the deepest canyons. So much rock: heaved up into mountains and mesas; split and gouged into arroyos, washes, and gulches so dark the sun never quite reaches the bottom; rock exposed by erosion and left open to view by the dry conditions that keep it largely uncovered. At times the plateau seems little more than a silent world of stone where life barely hangs on.

But more than rock lives on the plateau. Over geologic time, uplift and erosion have sculpted the rock into wildly diverse topographies, allowing an astonishing range of microclimates to flourish. In a single day a traveler on the plateau might traverse sun-baked deserts where it almost never rains, expansive flower-spangled grasslands, dense montane forests of spruce and aspen and fern, isolated alpine tundras ruled by wind, and the scattered oases, bejeweled green, of rivers and springs and marshes.

In all these environments life has intimately adapted itself to local conditions—aridity and moisture, heat and cold—in ways as multifarious as they are beautiful. It is simply elegant how aspen trees rely on forest fires to thrive, how the cryptobiotic crusts of the canyonlands both stabilize and enrich the dry soil, how piñon pines feed birds that in turn disperse the trees' seeds to places they could never reach on their own. The web of life is woven fine on the Colorado Plateau, and teasing apart its myriad connections is one of the great pleasures of living—or visiting—here.

SAND AND SLICKROCK

by Richard Mahler

Sandstone is not the only rock in the Southwest, but picturing the Colorado Plateau without it is like imagining Seattle without rain, or Minneapolis without winter. It is one of those natural features that immediately puts places into context—and sticks fast in the memory.

The region's sandstone is composed of ancient sand that eroded from other rocks eons ago. It provides a record of long-vanished climates, some of them wetter and some even drier than today's. Much of the reddish Entrada Sandstone exposed at Arches National Park was deposited on the beaches and tidal flats of a shallow prehistoric sea. In contrast, the cream- or orange-colored Navajo Sandstone that forms massive cliffs in Zion and Capitol Reef national parks forms a record of a Sahara-like desert, the huge dunes of which once covered a wide area.

Once buried by other sediments, these sands were cemented into rock. Over millions of years, the uplift of the Colorado Plateau and the action of erosion have caused many ancient sand deposits to reappear. When exposed, softer sections of rock are worn away by wind, rain, and frost, leaving harder rocks to form the arches, fins, towers, mesas, and alcoves so characteristic of the Southwest.

Sometimes the delicate ripples of ancient dunes, the large but fragile tracks of dinosaurs, or the imprints of fallen leaves are recorded on a sandstone surface. They are priceless records of the earth's pre-human past, exposed for just a blink of geological time before the rock crumbles and is free to drift again.

VOLCANOES

by Dennis Wall

The volcanic mountains of the Southwest are places of beauty and peace, perfect places for hiking and camping. But they have not always been so tranquil. At times, they have been places of chaos and fire.

Volcanoes of various sorts dot the Colorado Plateau. Some, such as the San Francisco Peaks north of Flagstaff, are stratovolcanoes built by innumerable extended eruptions over hundreds of thousands of years. Others are cinder cones, gray-black or brick-red, that formed during the course of much briefer eruptions.

Many of the fresh-looking lava flows in such places as El Malpais National Monument in New Mexico and Sunset Crater Volcano National Monument in Arizona spilled out during the same eruptions that formed cinder cones. Some of them are geological infants. One-thousand-foot-high Sunset Crater Volcano formed around the year 1064, and jagged lava flows at El Malpais may be even younger.

People were around to see these events. The eruptions no doubt created fear, but people benefited from them, too. After Sunset Crater Volcano formed, native people found that the new volcanic ash that coated the land for miles around the mountain served as natural mulch and improved crop yields.

Geologists believe that some of the Southwest's volcanic fields are still active and could erupt again. In some areas, small earthquakes occur periodically, but volcanologists do not expect eruptions anytime soon. During our tiny slice of geologic time, at least, volcanoes are beautiful oases of peace in a hectic world.

HOW CANYONS GROW

by Anne Minard

When a rock falls somewhere in the Grand Canyon, does a geologist hear it? Maybe not, but Bob Webb might still learn that it happened.

The basics of Grand Canyon geology might be summed up in six words: "River cuts down, sides fall in." Webb is a U.S. Geological Survey hydrologist who has long studied just how the sides fall in, often by comparing modern views with historic photographs. Such comparisons show how the canyon has changed.

Historically, the canyon walls have crumbled in two ways: through debris flows and rockfalls. Debris flows are loose slurries of mud, water, and rocks triggered by heavy rains. They course rapidly down channels and have formed most of the Colorado River's rapids. Perhaps the most famous was the enormous debris flow of December 1966, caused by some five inches of rain; the debris created the huge waves of Crystal Rapid.

Rockfalls occur more haphazardly, though they are perhaps most common during soaking winter storms. Geologists can predict which rock layers are most likely to crumble, but Webb says he doubts science will ever be able to predict when and where rockfalls are most likely to occur.

Falling rocks do pose dangers. Four members of a river trip had to be evacuated a few years ago after plummeting rocks landed on their tents, causing serious injuries. At least one river camp has been destroyed by a small debris flow; fortunately, the campers were out hiking when it happened, and no one was hurt. A little danger, after all, is a small price to pay for a wilderness experience in such a rocky and wild place.

THE POOP ON THE PLEISTOCENE

by Rose Houk

Jim Mead has a nose for old dung. As a paleontologist at Northern Arizona University, that's a useful gift. Mead sniffs out caves that contain the remains of ancient diets. If the deposits smell like a rich, aromatic wine and are a dull, earthy rust or brown in color, then they are likely to be more than five thousand years old—sometimes much older.

With its numerous dry alcoves and caves, the Colorado Plateau is a great place to look for petrified poop. Researchers have been examining the plateau's fossil dung since the 1930s, but the field got a great boost when Mead and colleague Larry Agenbroad discovered one particularly poopy cave in Glen Canyon National Recreation Area in 1983.

Bechan Cave turned out to be a sensational find. It held about three hundred cubic yards of dung—enough to fill a big front-end loader one hundred times. Nearly all of it was left behind by grass-eating mammoths some thirteen thousand years ago.

Fossil dung has also revealed that such now-extinct animals as the Shasta ground sloth, Harrington's mountain goat, and shrub oxen once lived on the plateau. Their partially digested meals reveal what plants they ate—and what the area looked like thousands of years ago.

On the plateau, all of these big mammals vanished twelve to thirteen thousand years ago. The cause, or causes, of that large-scale extinction are unclear: climate change, overkill by big-game hunters, and disease are the prime theories. We may never know for certain what happened—but maybe the knowledge gained with the aid of Jim Mead's nose will help us avoid future extinctions.

SEEPS AND SPRINGS

by Richard Mahler

Seeps and springs are lush green oases in southwestern deserts. Although they account for only a fraction of 1 percent of the surface area of the Southwest, they often support a density of life five hundred times greater than that found in surrounding terrain. Seeps and springs teem with mosses, algae, ferns, and other riparian flora, as well as insects, snails, frogs, birds, bats, and large mammals.

Some of these species are relics of the most recent ice age; they are making a last stand at these tiny islands of moisture. A few occur at a single spring and nowhere else on earth.

The presence of seeps and springs is dictated by cracks and faults in geologic formations. By studying the chemistry of the water that emerges, experts can sometimes determine how long ago it fell as rain or snow. In some cases, the water that bubbles up fell from the sky thousands of years ago.

Indigenous people left offerings at such places as gifts to the earth for its life-sustaining water. Larger springs were sometimes deepened or channeled to nurture crops or grow medicinal plants. But recent history has been less kind. Most springs that were running free and clear a century ago have since dried up, been piped away, or become contaminated. Deep wells threaten many of the remaining springs by lowering groundwater tables.

Water law in the southwestern states does little to restrict such wells. Reducing our reliance on groundwater by using water sparingly would help preserve these special places that are oases for so many wild creatures—and for the human spirit.

MONSOON POLLINATORS

by Peter Friederici

It begins with a few puffy, white clouds over the mountains and high mesas, builds up through increasingly humid and cloudy afternoons, and culminates in the lightning, thunder, and downpours of mighty storms.

At a time of year when much of the West gets drier by the day, the summer monsoon season in the Southwest initiates an explosion in biological productivity and diversity. Penstemons, sunflowers, gilias, Rocky Mountain bee plant, and many other plants thrive and bloom in the wake of drenching monsoon rains. The colors are magnificent: red, orange, yellow, blue, and purple. The pollinators they attract are beautiful as well.

Bees, hummingbirds, and moths visit these flowers to feed on nectar. As they sip, they inadvertently transfer pollen, fertilizing the flower's seeds and facilitating a new generation of plants.

Some of these pollinators are international travelers. For rufous hummingbirds, this is only one stop on a long migratory journey. In early spring these tiny, energetic birds work their way north through lowland deserts in the Southwest on their way to nesting sites in the Pacific Northwest. Looking like orange darts of flame, they zing around our high-country meadows during the monsoon season, gathering fuel for the long trip back to wintering sites in central and southern Mexico.

Such pollinators are a tangible tie to other places, and a reminder that conservation links animals and people in many different lands. This monsoon season, take a few minutes to watch the birds, bees, and butterflies as they gather their sweet reward and give us ours—and then wish them *buena suerte* on their journey.

CRYPTOBIOTIC CRUSTS

by Peter Friederici

There is a lot of open space in the arid Southwest. Trees and shrubs grow far apart, separated by what looks like bare ground.

But a closer look reveals that the ground is not bare at all. In many places it is covered with a dark, richly textured layer that is more solid than sand or dirt. Known as cryptobiotic crust, it thrives on the Colorado Plateau, where it often forms castle-like towers and pinnacles three inches high, like medieval cities in miniature.

Cryptobiotic crusts form when a combination of bacteria, fungi, lichens, and mosses grow together. When moisture comes, these organisms grow, and the bacteria and fungi leave behind long, tubular strands that help bind soil particles together.

Soil crusts hold water, reduce erosion, and deliver nutrients that larger plants need. Their dark color absorbs sunlight, warming the soil and allowing plants to grow earlier in the spring. Cryptobiotic crusts are key in supporting desert plant and animal life.

Unfortunately, crusts grow slowly and are easily destroyed by careless footsteps or off-road tire tracks. Because it takes decades for a trampled or crushed crust to renew itself, it is crucial for desert hikers, bikers, and drivers to stay on existing roads and trails. Remember: don't bust the crust! Admire these tiny but complex communities with your eyes only, and leave them healthy for others to enjoy.

ASPENS

by Richard Mahler

Whether bright lime-green in spring, brilliant yellow in autumn, or stark white in winter, quaking aspen trees always catch the eye. And they do so in many places. Aspens grow in northern Mexico, high in numerous western mountain ranges, and throughout the northern states, Canada, Europe, and Siberia. Aspens, in fact, are the most widespread trees in North America.

Aspens might be said to have a rock-and-roll life strategy: live fast and die young. They thrive most where fires or avalanches have killed off other trees. Aspen roots respond to sunlight warming the ground by sprouting vigorously, forming dense thickets of stems that are clones of one another.

These trees grow quickly but seldom live more than a century. Unless fire or another disturbance returns, they are usually crowded out by slower-growing but longer-living conifers such as spruce and fir trees.

While they are around, aspens attract a lot of attention, and not just from leaf-peepers. Because aspens allow dappled light to reach the ground, they are usually surrounded by lush grasses, wildflowers, and shrubs. Woodpeckers carve nest holes in the soft trunks. Beavers collect stems for winter food. And many animals feed on succulent aspen leaves and sometimes bark.

Due to swelling elk and deer populations, as well as widespread fire suppression, aspen groves have become less common in the West. Keeping them around may require some thoughtful management, such as controlling elk numbers and allowing some forest fires to burn. It makes sense to think about the future of aspens as we enjoy the beauty they give us in the present.

Piñon Pines

by Peter Friederici

Piñon pines are unassuming trees that grow slowly and never reach great heights. But they virtually define the Southwest. Their range extends north through Utah and Colorado, east to New Mexico, and west to California.

Piñon pinecones contain large, tasty seeds that are chock-full of fat and protein—in fact, they are a more concentrated energy source than chocolate. Birds, rodents, squirrels, bears, and many other animals gather large numbers of these seeds, often storing them to eat during the winter.

People, too, have long relied on piñon pines for food. That requires some planning, as the trees do not bear large seed crops every year. Usually a few cones are available in any given place each year, but large crops come along only every seven years or so. Then the picking is easy.

It takes some work to crack open the hard, inedible shell, but once released, piñon nuts can be used in a wide variety of recipes, from salads to pesto to cookies. Whether raw or roasted, they make a great snack.

Pick some up at the store in the fall, or, better yet, pick some of your own out in the Colorado Plateau's extensive piñon-juniper woodlands. The nutty, oily, wild taste is the quintessential flavor of the Southwest.

PLACE

Part Two
People and Place

The rocks are laboriously pecked with drawings, chipped into fluted arrowheads, or stacked into buildings ancient or modern—and what they reveal is that people have lived here for a long time. That has meant much more, in times ancient or modern, than simply admiring the scenery. Since the end of the last ice age, people on the plateau have intimately engaged themselves with their surroundings—their place. They—we—have set fires to keep forests open and healthy, moved plants around, built houses from local materials, learned how to hunt or raise or admire animals, marked the places best suited for watching the stars.

It has not been easy. Face it: this is a tough, unforgiving environment. Often it does not rain enough to support the crops or the animals; then, when the rain clouds come, they release great torrents that crash off the high places in flash floods. Or fire comes, not corralled in one of the forms in which we can use it, but wild, uncontrolled, unpredictable.

Living in a region of such extremes demands close attention to flood and fire and rain, and to the suite of creatures that live here, including the people of the area's diverse cultures. It is by learning how the place works that people have been able to create the most elegant solutions to the difficulties of living here—and some of those solutions have been part of the Colorado Plateau for a long, long time.

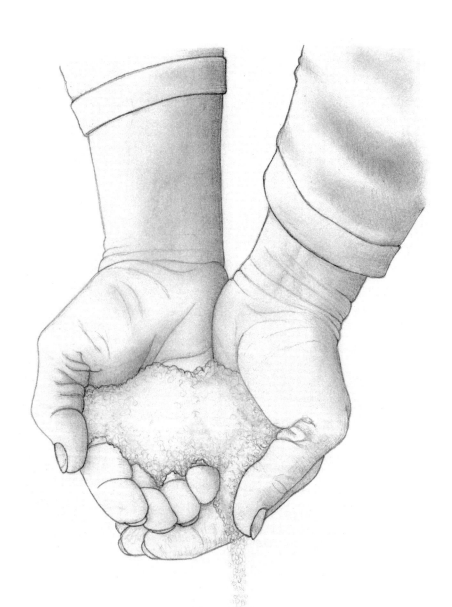

SALT

by Richard Mahler

For most of us, salt is a simple condiment that rarely merits a second thought. But to the indigenous people of the Southwest, salt has long been of critical importance—and not simply as a trade item, seasoning, or preservative.

For the Hopi people of northeastern Arizona, salt-gathering trips to natural deposits in the Grand Canyon have long been strenuous and sacred rituals. Only men with sufficient knowledge of Hopi traditions are allowed on such journeys, since specific ceremonies need to be performed en route. A traveler's mind must be pure, his heart in harmony with the universe.

Hopis believe that the gathering of salt supports the growth of corn and the arrival of rain. They believe salt was deliberately put in a difficult place to remind them of its preciousness. The Hopi salt mines, located near the confluence of the Colorado and Little Colorado rivers, have been placed off-limits by the National Park Service out of respect for the tribe.

The Hopi, in turn, supported the Zuni people in opposing a proposed coal mine near Zuni Salt Lake in western New Mexico. For these and many other tribes, this deposit has long been a sacred pilgrimage destination and a place of peace where conflicts are set aside. The Zuni regard salt gathered here as the flesh of Salt Mother, an important deity who helps maintain balance and health within the tribe. The coal mine project was ultimately canceled, a decision in line with native beliefs that salt is a gift of the earth, to be regarded with the utmost respect.

CALENDARS OF STONE

by Bryan Bates

For most of us, May Day is not a major holiday. But for people a millennium ago it was a time of year that held great significance. May Day is one of four days that fall halfway between a solstice and an equinox. These days mark the times when the length of the days begins to change most dramatically.

On May 1 the sun itself marks this event by rising in the center of a small portal in an ancient solar calendar wall at Wupatki National Monument in northern Arizona. This solar calendar is one of several that have been identified in the Four Corners region. It is believed that it served both practical and ceremonial purposes.

Portals at Wupatki mark three different days of astronomical significance. The first corresponds to the modern Groundhog Day in midwinter. May Day is the second. The third marks a day shortly after the summer solstice. For the Hopi, that day indicates that the Kachinas will soon bring life-giving monsoon rains from the direction of the San Francisco Peaks.

For Hopi farmers, the beginning of May is the time for planting corn, squash, and beans. It is possible that farmers of a thousand years ago used the Wupatki calendar to tell them when to plant.

Ancient peoples did not have paper calendars or newspapers to tell them what day it was. But in spring, as we enjoy the days getting longer, our feeling of rebirth probably is not that different from what they felt in looking at their precise stone calendars.

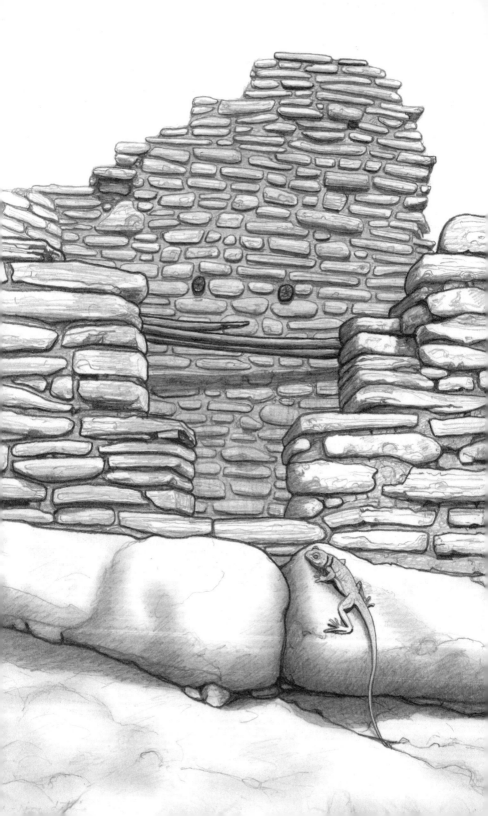

CHANGES IN THE WEATHER

by Mary Tolan

Old-timers know that the climate of the Southwest shifts dramatically from wet to dry and back again. Recent archaeological research has shown that these shifts have affected human life for centuries.

When U.S. Highway 89 north of Flagstaff was widened around the turn of the twenty-first century, archaeologists found numerous pit houses along its route. By examining tree rings in the house beams, they have been able to precisely date the structures. The rings also reveal what the climate was like when those trees grew more than nine centuries ago.

As a result, we now know that the ancient Sinagua and Cohonina people lived near the San Francisco Peaks when the climate was hot and dry, but moved into the lower piñon-juniper zone when conditions were wetter.

Such climate shifts last longer than the well-known El Niño and La Niña events, which tend to linger only a few years. The Pacific Decadal Oscillation, for example, is a twenty- to thirty-year climate cycle related to water temperatures in the northwest Pacific Ocean. That water has been getting warmer, which may favor a long dry spell. And some shifts are even longer term: tree rings show that the Southwest's climate has been relatively wet in the last two hundred years—and especially moist in the last twenty. Drier conditions may resemble what the area experienced in the past.

We may not move around in response to climate shifts as the ancients did. But maybe we can learn from them that such changes are a part of life here, and that the ability to adapt to change is an important skill in an arid land.

GRIZZLY BEARS

by Mona Mort

Whatever people feel about grizzly bears, everyone agrees that spending time in their territory makes people more aware of their surroundings. As recently as 1850, these giant omnivores roamed throughout much of western North America. Some lived on the Colorado Plateau.

Grizzlies like many foods besides meat, such as berries and acorns. But because they do eat meat, early ranchers saw them as competitors, and the federal government paid hunters to kill them. In the 1880s, one hunter named Bear Howard built a cabin in Arizona's Oak Creek Canyon and set to work. He earned ten dollars for a grizzly bear scalp, twenty for a pelt. The meat sold on the chopping block.

Bear Howard and other hunters did their work all too well. In 1935 the last grizzly in Arizona was killed in Strayhorse Canyon in eastern Arizona. As late as 1979 a grizzly was shot in southwestern Colorado's San Juan Mountains, and some believe a few of the great bears may linger there. They still roam the northern Rocky Mountains, western Canada, and Alaska. Although the bears remain unpopular with many ranchers, they are protected under the Endangered Species Act.

The great naturalist Aldo Leopold described the shooting of the last grizzly on Escudilla Mountain in eastern Arizona. "It's only a mountain now," he wrote. Grizzlies may not be returning to the Colorado Plateau anytime soon, but we can respect their memory by living in harmony with the rest of the region's animals.

Apaches and Wolves

by Peter Friederici

Not too long ago, the Apache people and Mexican wolves shared the rugged lands of central Arizona and New Mexico. Apache warriors sometimes recited a ritual song before they went out to fight. "Let me be powerful like the wolf," they sang.

The arrival of new settlers from the east changed everything. The Apache people were restricted to reservations, and the wolves were wiped out to protect big game for hunters and the cattle of ranchers. Only a few survived in zoos.

Fortunately, that is not the end of the story. In 1998 federal biologists began releasing captive-bred Mexican wolves in far eastern Arizona and western New Mexico. The wolves have successfully hunted and reared young. By preying on abundant elk and deer, they are helping to restore an ecological balance. But many have been illegally shot or struck by cars in their national forest homes, which are popular with hunters and campers.

Arizona's White Mountain Apache Tribe has formally agreed to allow wild wolves back on its extensive lands. That decision gives the wolves more room to roam in places where they will encounter fewer people and cars. It also represents the rebirth of a cultural link. At the official signing of the agreement to welcome back wolves, an Apache musician once again sang the traditional wolf song, which had been forgotten by all but a few tribal elders.

Tribal officials hope that the wolf's presence will result in new economic opportunities, such as ecotourism or the marketing of predator-friendly beef. Thanks to the persistence of a few people—and a few wolves—an ancient tradition of coexistence is continuing in a new millennium.

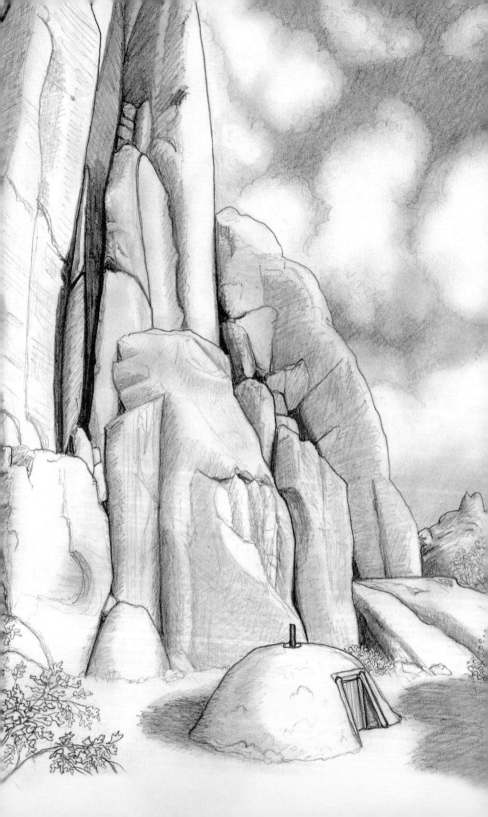

Hogans

by Richard Mahler

We see them scattered throughout parts of Arizona, Utah, and New Mexico: the small, often windowless hogans that are the traditional homes of the Navajo people, or Diné. The Navajo creation story relates how the first hogan was built of forked and straight logs by Coyote, with the help of Beaver, soon after humans emerged from underground.

Although the design has been modified over the years, the basic elements remain the same. A hogan's entrance always faces east, so that its occupants can properly greet the dawn. Men sit inside on the south side, women on the north, and important guests at the west, a place of honor. Once inside, everyone moves clockwise, following the sun.

Traditionally, a certain type and number of logs were used in a hogan's walls. A round hogan covered with packed mud was considered female. Male hogans looked something like pyramids, with triangular walls.

After the arrival of the railroad in the late nineteenth century, the traditional five-sided hogan was modified through the use of abandoned railroad ties. Today's hogans are larger and may have six or eight sides.

The symbolism of these buildings remains vital to traditional Navajos, who always maintain a hogan for ceremonies, healing, and balance, even if they live in a modern house. Sacred traditions are also maintained in public buildings such as schools and offices, the shapes of which sometimes suggest a hogan. For the Navajo people, a hogan is not simply a home; it reflects the intimate relationship between a people, their culture, and the environment.

FIRE LOOKOUTS

by Mike Lamp

Our national forests feature spectacular scenery. No one has a better view than the people who spend their summers as fire lookouts.

From towers in places like Kendrick Peak near Flagstaff and Park Peak in Colorado's Mesa Verde National Park lookouts may survey a thousand square miles. Always watchful for threads of smoke, they also notice light and shadows moving across mountains and forests.

Granted weeks of almost unbroken solitude, these mountaintop sentinels have time to consider interior landscapes. Some well-known writers have found inspiration in lookout cabins. Jack Kerouac and Gary Snyder wrote of their adventures and impressions as lookouts in Washington State. Edward Abbey took in the view from a tower on the North Rim of the Grand Canyon, and he integrated what he called "a sea of treetops" and the song of the hermit thrush into his essays and novels.

Fifty years ago there were some eight thousand lookouts on duty across the country. That number has been shrinking as aircraft and satellites now help locate fires. These days about a thousand lookouts are working nationwide. Often they keep watch on the prescribed fires set to maintain forest health.

Some towers that are no longer needed, meanwhile, have been opened for vacation rentals. They are popular with wilderness lovers who like heights and long views.

Many lookouts who continue to work today have been at their jobs for many years, even decades. It is not hard to understand why. As one Colorado lookout has said, "You get up there and the whole world is yours."

STEAM HEAT

by Rose Houk

Energy efficiency is in the news today, but it is not really new. For decades, buildings in one southwestern city were heated by plentiful, locally produced energy. The source was steam from a local utility, the Flagstaff Electric Light Company. Sawdust, wood chips, and other wood waste from a local lumber mill fed the company's electrical boilers. The steam had just gone up the stack for years, until someone thought to put it to good use.

In 1920 the *Northern Arizona Leader* crowed that: "after the first of next October the merchant in Flagstaff can turn on the heat as easily as he now turns on his lights . . . the friendly old stove that scorched your coat tails when you were not noticing . . . will be a thing of the past."

The steam mains ran through underground concrete tunnels. The steam was piped into radiators in each building, and condensed water was cycled back from the radiators. At one time, more than one hundred customers were heating homes and businesses through the system.

Centralized power plants and natural gas heat put an end to Flagstaff's steam heat system. These days, few people know the comforting clanking of radiators—the sound of a locally generated, closed system that today bears the fancy name of "cogeneration." But some are considering new power systems that would use the abundant small trees of the Southwest to produce electricity—and perhaps steam heat, too. By generating electricity and heat locally, we might indeed go back to the future.

Preserving Chimayó's Potreros

by Richard Mahler

When many of us hear the word "conservation," we think about protecting what is most wild, such as national parks, forests, and wilderness areas. This definition is accurate, but limited; these days conservation applies increasingly to lands shaped by people, too.

A case in point is the northern New Mexico village of Chimayó, site of a famous nineteenth-century chapel, or *santuario*. Each year the Santuario de Chimayó attracts nearly three hundred thousand visitors. Many go inside the old adobe sanctuary to gather holy dirt, which is said to have miraculous healing powers. Some pilgrims swear the sacred soil cures chronic ailments, or at least eases their pain.

Behind the santuario are lush irrigated pastures—*potreros* in Spanish—where animals have grazed and crops have grown for more than two centuries. Traditionally, such lands have provided much of Chimayó's food. Today, however, rising land prices and job demands have prompted many residents to sell their pastures, gardens, and orchards to developers, who often convert them into lots for homes.

With the help of landowners and the local government, the potreros behind the Santuario de Chimayó have been rescued from development by the Trust for Public Land, which arranged for their purchase as county open space. The nonprofit group argued that modern housing would clash with the natural peace of the santuario, and that destruction of the pastures would threaten cultural values and end six generations of careful stewardship.

For decades Chimayó's farmers have promoted self-reliance, a serene ambiance, and a healthy local ecosystem. Now they will be able to pass that tradition on to new generations.

PART THREE

LIVING WITH
AN EYE ON THE FUTURE

Modern technology has disguised the extent to which our civilization is dependent upon particular places. The challenges of living in an arid environment, though, are still formidable. We all need to drink water and to eat food. We all need to nurture plants, animals, children, and communities. We need the sustenance—physical and psychological—provided by healthy and diverse natural surroundings. And, in an era when humans appear to be changing the very climate we live in, it is in our best interest to be acutely aware of how much fuel is expended in hauling our food and building materials to local stores.

The interconnections that tie plant to animal to people, after all, do not end at the edge of the Colorado Plateau. Rather, they extend all over the earth through its climate patterns, its migrating animals, its air currents, its flows of energy.

It is partly to ensure that those interconnections remain healthy that ever-increasing numbers of people on the plateau and elsewhere are channeling their energies into varied practices of sustainability. They are using techniques old and new: they are building houses with renewable resources, reintroducing endangered animals, raising heirloom vegetables or native grasses in gardens, watching hawks, turning the lights down. They represent a groundswell of good, workable ideas aimed at one goal: ensuring that our grandchildren, and their children, have the same opportunities to experience the diverse and beautiful land of rocks that is the Colorado Plateau just as we can enjoy it today.

RETURN OF THE CONDORS

by Anne Minard

Once upon a time, pink-headed, hunchbacked California condors crisscrossed the skies over much of North America, looking for dead bison, beached whales, and other carrion to eat. Condor bones and even petrified eggshells have been found in Grand Canyon caves, proving that the giant scavengers lived and nested there.

But condor numbers crashed in the twentieth century. Collisions with power lines, illegal shooting, egg collecting, and lead poisoning all played a part. The last northern Arizona sighting came near Williams, south of the Grand Canyon, in 1924. In the late 1980s, scientists in southern California trapped the remaining wild condors and placed them in a captive-breeding program.

The program worked. In 1992 biologists began releasing young captive-bred condors in California. The Grand Canyon, too, hosts newly wild condors. The nonprofit Peregrine Fund, in cooperation with other organizations, has been releasing condors at cliffs north of the canyon since 1996.

It is not easy preparing these birds for the wild. Biologists feed them carrion when necessary and monitor behavioral cues to determine when the birds are ready for release. The scientists do their work from a distance, so the birds do not become accustomed to people.

The hard work seems to have paid off. Condors released in northern Arizona have explored areas as far afield as Colorado, Wyoming, and western Arizona, and they have proven capable of finding their own food. They have also shown an interest in mating. In late 2003 a wild-hatched condor finally took its first flight from a Grand Canyon cave. It was a small step for that bird, but a giant leap for the species. Two additional condors fledged in northern Arizona in 2004. Keep your eyes open as you explore canyon country: you might see a condor overhead, soaring without effort on wings broader than an eagle's.

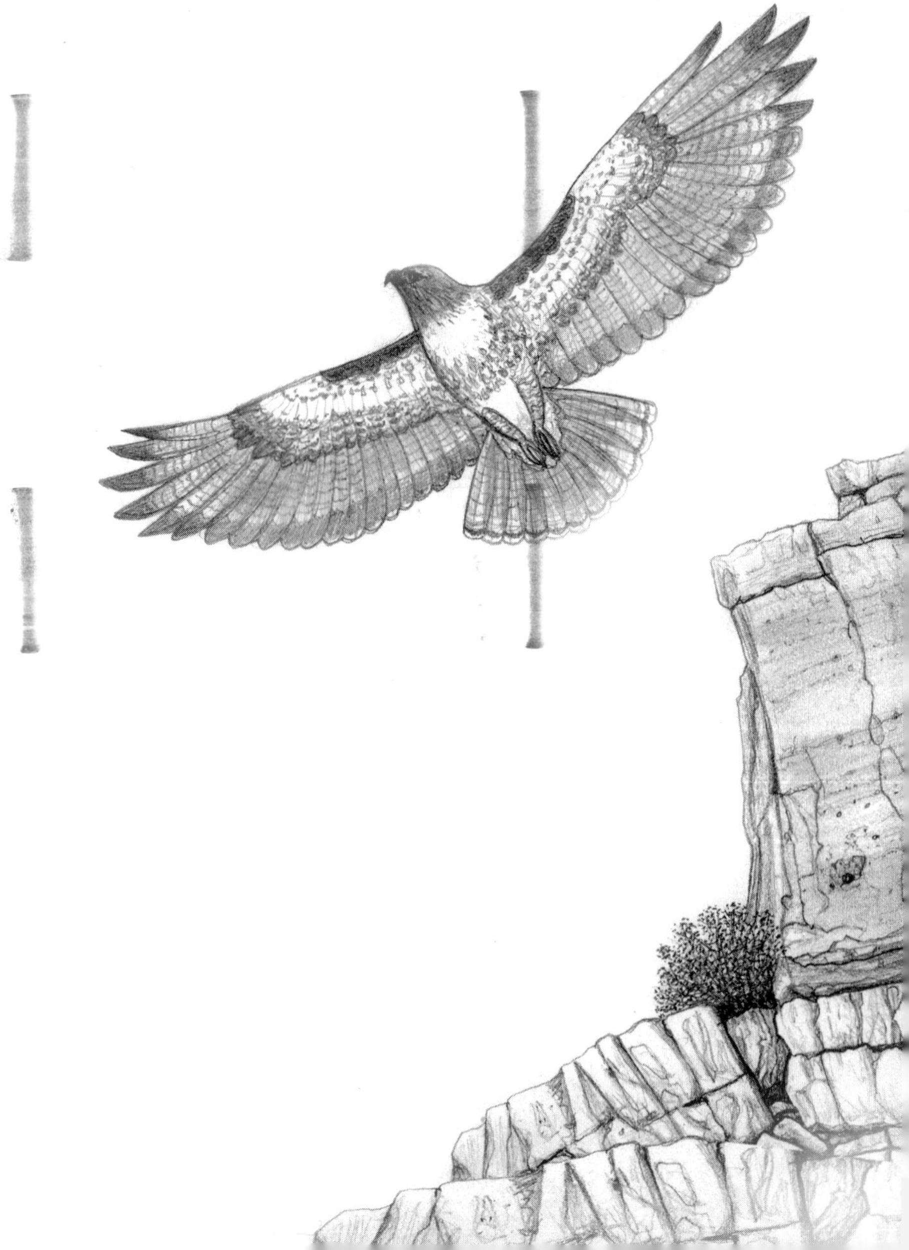

GRAND CANYON HAWKS

by John Grahame

In 1987 northern Arizona field biologist Chuck LaRue made a grand discovery: the massive fall migration of hawks and other raptors along the intermountain migratory flyway from Alaska to Mexico streams right over the Grand Canyon. Since that eye-opener, the nonprofit organization HawkWatch International has systematically counted the birds each fall from Lipan and Yaki points on the canyon's South Rim.

The migration season lasts from late August to early November. During a typical year observers may count over ten thousand red-tailed, Cooper's, and sharp-shinned hawks, along with up to sixteen other raptor species, as they are lifted out of the canyon by strong thermals and updrafts.

It is a rare treat to watch hawks and eagles rising upward from the canyon depths. And thanks to the years of monitoring that have already taken place, ornithologists are able to track long-term trends in the populations of these keystone predators.

HawkWatch International welcomes participation in its Grand Canyon project from experienced birders, but you do not have to be an ornithologist to check out the action. The field crews now include trained educators who greet visitors, explain the project, and conduct regular programs on raptor migration and identification. A similar program is underway in the Manzano Mountains southeast of Albuquerque.

At the canyon, sightings peak between late September and early October. Ask a park ranger to direct you to the observation points, and you could see dozens of America's most impressive birds riding the airwaves across one of the world's prettiest landscapes.

KEEPING PHANTOM RANCH CLEAN

by Terri Likens

What goes down must come up. It is not just a rule of physics, but a matter of policy at Grand Canyon's Phantom Ranch.

Every morning, a team of ten or so supply-laden mules heads down the steep switchbacks of the South Kaibab Trail to the remote lodge on the canyon's floor, nearly a mile below the rim. Every day, the mules make the climb back up and out, this time packing garbage and neatly separated recyclables.

Keeping the ranch's emerald-green oasis and the surrounding habitat clean is a priority for both the National Park Service and the Xanterra ranch staff. Every year, about seventy thousand visitors backpack down from the canyon rims, visit by mule, or raft to the river landing a half mile from Phantom Ranch. They drink at the dining hall and eat everything from steak to stew. Along the way they generate plenty of garbage.

How that garbage is dealt with is a matter of pride. Phantom Ranch workers say that they separate for recycling 50 percent of the waste generated. Other waste is reused on site. Eggshells and uneaten fruits and vegetables are composted at the ranch, then mixed with mule manure. The nutrient-rich mix is used to nourish plants in the developed area.

You probably will not see mules instead of garbage trucks on your hometown streets anytime soon. But simply throwing most garbage away does not work any better in the landscape at large than it would in the canyon. Just think: if recycling can work in a place as out of the way as Phantom Ranch, it can certainly work in our towns and cities. All it takes is a little commitment.

HEIRLOOM SEEDS

by Richard Mahler

Everyone knows that much of our food comes from plants. And plants, of course, grow from seeds. But where do seeds come from?

The question is important because relying too much on only a few varieties of seeds makes our food supply highly vulnerable to disease, insect damage, and climate change. The security of our food supply depends on genetic diversity. That diversity is threatened. So-called "heirloom" crops such as Taos Red and Four Corners Gold beans, native to the Colorado Plateau, are repositories of genetic variation. The Colorado Plateau is rich in heirloom corn, beans, gourds, sunflowers, and tobaccos, but it has also lost many varieties through neglect and widespread use of only a few hybrid crops.

Now a widespread movement is underway to cultivate heirloom varieties and grow these seeds on a regular basis as insurance for the future. Hopi farmers in the Arizona village of Sipaulovi are reviving historic apricot, peach, melon, and squash varieties. But others can contribute to this tradition of diversity, too.

It makes sense to do so. Heirloom varieties are usually better adapted to drought and other local conditions than commercial varieties. They often taste better. As more people grow them, their irreplaceable genetic material is more likely to be preserved. Such seeds are available from groups such as Tucson's Native Seeds/SEARCH, which has preserved over two thousand crop varieties from Mexico and the southwestern states.

Heirloom seeds reflect the ancient wisdom of indigenous farmers. Collecting and growing them helps preserve important food sources and cultural traditions.

Rescuing the Razorback Sucker

by Terri Likens

Before they were tamed by dams, the Colorado River and its tributaries raged with muddy floods in spring and summer, and sometimes turned to mere trickles in the fall. Unique native fishes thrived in these harsh and highly variable conditions.

One, the razorback sucker, has a prominent hump on its back that allows it to navigate in turbulent water. In the early twentieth century, the razorback was so abundant that it was fished commercially. But now this species is in trouble, due to extreme alterations of its river habitat, as well as competition with or predation by nonnative species such as bass and catfish.

Almost all the razorbacks that are left are growing old. Most probably hatched either before or soon after the Colorado's major dams were built. When they spawn, most of their eggs and young are eaten by nonnative predators.

Worried about the species' survival, biologists and officials from state and federal agencies are working to preserve the razorback. In the spring, volunteers with dip nets capture newly hatched razorbacks only a half inch long. The fish are transferred to a hatchery, and later they are moved to protected backwaters along the lower Colorado and ponds elsewhere. After growing in these safe environments for a year, they are released back into the main reservoir. Bigger and stronger, they stand a better chance against predators.

This is only a stopgap measure—but it is helping to keep the species alive until we can figure out whether it is possible to control nonnative species and restore southwestern rivers to something like what they once were.

Rebuilding Adobes

by Mona Mort

Cultural transmission. That is the term anthropologists use for the ways in which people pass on tips for survival—and for fun—from one generation to the next. It works best when the advice comes in one's younger years. That is why Cornerstones, a nonprofit organization based in Santa Fe, trains youths in traditional building skills.

Cornerstones strives to preserve cultural heritage and build community pride by restoring historic buildings—and using traditional construction methods—in the southwestern states. One project at the Pueblo of Acoma in western New Mexico, for example, involved constructing a model four-bedroom adobe home that provides much-needed housing on the reservation.

Most of the trainees had no previous construction experience. They came to the project only with a desire to learn the building techniques of their grandfathers. They left with an array of new hands-on skills and with an increased appreciation of their cultural history.

Cornerstones also helps to preserve and restore historic adobe structures, often with workdays that mingle local residents with other volunteers. Carefully plastering a fresh coat of mud on a historic adobe church can extend its life for decades, and the work is a great way to get in touch with the past. At Acoma, one of the historic buildings that has been restored is the grand old San Esteban del Rey Church and Convent. It now overlooks other adobe buildings, old and new, throughout the pueblo, and links the traditional past with a future based on those venerable traditions.

Building with Straw

by Richard Mahler

Remember the three little pigs? The idea of making walls out of such cheap, common, and flimsy material as straw might seem a fairy tale. But innovative builders—especially in the dry climate of the Southwest—have begun using ordinary straw to construct safe, sturdy, environmentally friendly, beautiful dwellings.

Straw bale houses are easy to build with the help of friends or professional workers. The bales themselves are not exposed to the elements; they are covered with plaster or stucco inside and out. This prevents the straw from decomposing and keeps rodents away. Support beams help carry the weight of roofs and windows.

Straw bales provide insulation values two or three times higher than traditional wood-frame buildings with fiberglass insulation. The massive walls allow beautiful sculpting, minimize the transmission of noise, and moderate indoor temperature fluctuations year-round. Over the life of a straw bale home, energy needs are reduced by up to 80 percent.

Because straw is so widely available, the cost of transportation to building sites is usually minimal. As a result, it generally takes less energy (expended through the transportation of the bales) to build a straw bale house than one made of traditional materials.

In a broader sense, straw bale homes help our environment because they provide a good use for what is often a waste product. An estimated four hundred billion pounds of straw are burned in the United States each year, accounting for a fair portion of the country's carbon dioxide emissions. Using this material for building can help us cut back on our lumber needs and clear our air—and that's no fairy tale.

Just Bad Luck?

by Mike Lamp

Everyone knows you are supposed to take nothing but pictures at national parks. But a few visitors cannot resist a "souvenir." Some of them end up regretting it.

Rangers at Petrified Forest National Park in Arizona remind people that rock hunting is illegal and threatens the beauty of the park. Still, the park service estimates that visitors make off with a ton of petrified wood every month. Now and then a few pieces come back with letters that relate unusual occurrences of bad luck—or is it something more?

A woman who signed herself "Ashamed in Alabama" returned her stolen souvenir with a tale of lost jewelry and a serious car accident. Another woman told of getting home from the park to face car trouble and medical problems. "Then," she wrote, "our dog died."

"To whom it may concern," yet another letter begins. "I took these rocks from your park just to see if it was true that it would bring bad luck. I had heard that, but didn't believe it. Well, I believe it now—keep them, please!"

It might be just coincidence that misfortune follows pilfering. But the same thing happens elsewhere in the Southwest, such as at Chaco Culture National Historical Park in northern New Mexico. Rangers there get apologies and sad stories from visitors sending back stolen potsherds and other artifacts of ancestral Puebloan culture.

When you visit these parks, enjoy the letters on display at the visitor centers. They are there for future visitors to appreciate—the same reason the ancient resources of those parks must remain.

Keeping the Night Sky Dark

by Peter Friederici

The night sky has always been an awe-inspiring sight. On a dark night, the endless expanse of black velvet is studded with more stars than anyone can count—a breathtaking glimpse of the universe.

In most cities and towns, though, night skies are no longer dark. A thousand points of light pollution spill into the sky from brightly lit streets, businesses, and homes, obscuring the stars and turning the black sky orange. Today, a typical suburban sky is five to ten times brighter than the natural sky.

All that wasted electric light costs at least 1.5 billion dollars a year nationwide. It has made it more difficult for astronomers in observatories to use their telescopes—and the rest of us are losing the best free show in town.

Fortunately, this is the easiest kind of pollution to fix. Some western towns and cities are reducing light pollution with stringent lighting codes, but citizens have to do their part, too. It's easy: just turn off yard and porch lights when it is time for bed, or install motion-sensing lights that switch off when no one is around. You can also buy shielded light fixtures that cast light toward the ground, where it is needed, and not up into the sky. By preventing light pollution, you will be saving on your electric bill, too.

Remember: stars up, lights down. With just a little bit of effort from all of us, we can keep our electric light on the ground and leave the sky to the stars.

PUBLISHING PARTNERS

KNAU

KNAU engages listeners with distinctive radio programming. Northern Arizona University's public radio service operates transmitters in Flagstaff, Prescott, Grand Canyon, Show Low, Kingman, Page, and Cottonwood, with main studios on the NAU campus in Flagstaff. KNAU's 100,000-watt Flagstaff station broadcasts at 88.7 FM. The Arizona Public Radio network is recognized as one of National Public Radio's leading rural radio services; its station reporters frequently contribute to NPR newsmagazines. KNAU offers two program services: NPR news and classical music, and NPR news and talk. Northern Arizona residents, businesses, and organizations generously support KNAU with financial contributions and program underwriting. Find out more about KNAU at http://www.knau.org, where live and archived station audio is available. *Earth Notes* debuted on KNAU in January 2001.

Center for Sustainable Environments

Northern Arizona University's Center for Sustainable Environments is a catalyst for collaborative research, education, training, and stewardship among its diverse partners. It brings together the talents and expertise of scientists, educators, independent scholars, business leaders, government agencies, nonprofit organizations, students, and community members to seek creative solutions to environmental problems. These challenges are addressed through initiatives that safeguard natural and cultural values and resources. By combining technical innovations with the knowledge, values, and practices of local communities, the center generates long-term environmental solutions that enhance the lives of those they impact. Read about the CSE's current projects at http://www.environment.nau.edu.

Grand Canyon Association

The Grand Canyon Association is a nonprofit, membership organization established in 1932 to support education and other programs for the benefit of Grand Canyon National Park and its visitors. GCA operates bookstores throughout the park, publishes books and other materials related to the Grand Canyon region, and produces a wide variety of free publications and exhibits for park visitors. GCA also supports scientific and cultural research, and funds acquisitions for the park's research library. In addition, through the Grand Canyon Field Institute, GCA operates hands-on, experiential trips into the park. Since 1932 GCA has provided Grand Canyon National Park with over $23 million in financial support. For more information, visit http://www.grandcanyon.org.

Transcripts and audio files of *Earth Notes* programs, along with links to more information, are available on the World Wide Web at http:www.earthnotesradio.org.

ABOUT THE
CONTRIBUTORS

Bryan Bates is a Flagstaff-based naturalist and science instructor with a personal and professional interest in archaeoastronomy.

Earth Notes editor **Peter Friederici** is a writer who lives in Flagstaff. He has published numerous books and magazine articles about nature and the environment.

John Grahame produces material for the Web, video, print, and radio. However, as a media consumer, he still prefers words, spoken or read. He chooses to live in Flagstaff against all odds.

Earth Notes developer and contributor **Rose Houk** is a freelance writer based in Flagstaff. She travels frequently on the Colorado Plateau, writing about natural history, archaeology, and human history.

Mike Lamp has been a contributor to National Public Radio, as well as a reporter and news host at NPR stations in Flagstaff and Denver.

Terri Likens has seen California condors in flight, felt the tickle of tarantula legs across bare skin, and snorkeled with rare native fish in Fossil Creek. A former Associated Press reporter, she has freelanced for *Plateau Journal*, *High Country News*, the *Arizona Republic*, ABCNews.com, and *American Profile*.

Richard Mahler is an independent writer and radio producer specializing in nature, conservation, and health. A longtime National Public Radio contributor, he has written for *Outside*, *EcoTraveler*, *Great Expeditions*, *New Mexico*, *Arizona Highways*, the *Los Angeles Times*, and dozens of other publications. Mahler's ten books include *Belize: Adventures in Nature* and *New Mexico's Best*.

Anne Minard is a freelance writer in Flagstaff who has written for a number of publications and media outlets, including the *New York Times*, *Science*, *High Country News*, and KNAU.

Mona Mort conveys science and technology in language everyone can understand. She has written over ninety articles for print, radio, and Web sites, and she is the author of *Verbatim: A Conversation with Charles Bowden*. Born in Arizona, raised in Michigan, Mona now lives and writes in Tucson.

The author of numerous works of natural history and ethnobotany, **Gary Paul Nabhan** directs the Center for Sustainable Environments at Northern Arizona University.

Mary Tolan has lived and written in the Southwest for more than twenty years. In addition to being a staff reporter and columnist for daily and weekly newspapers, she has freelanced for magazines and newspapers throughout the country. She has been teaching journalism at Northern Arizona University since 2002.

Dennis Wall is a freelance writer-photographer whose work has appeared in more than forty publications, including *Southwest Art*, *Popular Mechanics*, *New Mexico Magazine*, and many others. The author of the book *Western National Wildlife Refuges*, he currently serves as editor for the Institute for Tribal Environmental Professionals at Northern Arizona University.

PUBLIC RADIO
STATIONS HOSTING

Earth
N O T E S

88.1 KUYI Hotevilla, Ariz.

89.9 KUNM Albuquerque, N.Mex.

88.7 KNAU Flagstaff, Ariz.

89.3 KNAQ Prescott, Ariz.

89.5 KGHR Tuba City, Ariz.

89.7 KNAU Kingman, Ariz.

90.3 KNAG Grand Canyon, Ariz.

90.7 KNAA Show Low, Ariz.

91.7 KPUB Flagstaff, Ariz.

91.7 KNAD Page, Ariz.